寻找流浪的星星
searching for wandering stars

陈 伯 仑
CHEN BORLUEN

寻找流浪的星星
陈伯仑

版权 © 2021 – 陈华生. 版权所有

英文翻译: 陈华生, Satya Senesac, Sarah Simmonds.

国际标准书号: 978-1-7375241-0-6

联系作者: *bolun0405@gmail.com*

主编: 陈华生 – *kyraxe@hotmail.com*
封面设计: 陈力生
内容编排: Luca Funari – *funariediting@gmail.com*

Searching for Wandering Stars
Chen Borluen

Copyright © 2021 – Michael H. Chen. All Rights Reserved.

English Translation: Michael H. Chen, Satya Senesac, and Sarah Simmonds.

ISBN: 978-1-7375241-0-6

To contact the author: *bolun0405@gmail.com*

Chief Editor: Michael H. Chen – *kyraxe@hotmail.com*
Cover Illustration and Design: Sebastian Chen
Interior Layout: Luca Funari – *funariediting@gmail.com*

目录

简短序文 8
简介 10
致谢 12

诗篇 14

    一只小鸟 17
    秋叶 21
    木棉花开的季节 27
    四月天 31
    思念 35
    足 迹 41
    夕阳红 45
    大地震 49
    无奈 55
    梦幻 59
    妳为什么走了 63
    团圆 69
    失去的青春 73
    泡沫 77
    暮岁 81

Table of Contents

Preface..9
Brief Biography..11
Acknowledgements...13

Poems...15

    A Little Bird...17
    Autumn Leaves..21
    Kapok Season...27
    April Day..31
    Longing...35
    Footprints...41
    Red Sunset...45
    Catastrophic Earthquake..49
    Apathy..55
    Fantastical Dream...59
    Why Did You Leave Us..63
    Reunion..69
    Lost Youth..73
    Foam...77
    Twilight Years..81

燕子,飞走吧!	85
青藏高原	89
涟漪波纹	93
初雪	97
山火	101
交会	105
洛矶山群	109
永恒的真理	115
天山雪莲	119
树苗棚	123
暴风雪	129
天塌了	133
亲情	137
小烛光	141
无声之歌	145

Swallow, Fly Away!.................................85
The Qinghai-Tibet Plateau........................89
Ripples and Waves..................................93
Early Snow..97
Mountain Fire...101
Rendezvous..105
The Rocky Mountains.............................109
Eternal Truth..115
The Tianshan Snow Lotus.......................119
Greenhouse..123
Snowstorm...129
The Sky Has Collapsed...........................133
Family Affection.....................................137
Tiny Candles..141
Silent Song...145

简短序文

这本诗集是汇编了我的部分诗和绘画作品。我从过去25年里创作的作品中选择了30件与读者分享 - 其中许多作品已在多家网站和报纸上发表过。这些诗和绘画只是我的经历、思想、情感、灵感和想象力的点滴。

"寻找流浪的星星"是学习英语或汉语的中学生和大学生的理想读物,也是睡前阅读的好伴侣。欣赏优美的诗画,让人不知不觉坠入梦乡。

请访问下面网站,*https://chenbolun.wixsite.com/nanhaipoetrypainting*,可以获得视听读全面的体验。在该网站上您可以找到诗、画以及精选的音乐,从而获得非常独特的体验。

Preface

This book is a collection of my poetry and digital illustrations. I have selected 30 pieces from works I have created over the past 25 years to share with readers—many of which have been published on various websites and newspapers. These poems and paintings are just droplets of my experiences, thoughts, emotions, inspirations, and imagination.

"Searching for Wandering Stars" is ideal reading material for high school and university students who are studying English or Chinese. It is also a good companion at bedtime, allowing one to appreciate some poetry and artwork before unwittingly falling into the world of dreams.

For a more immersive experience, please visit *https://chenbolun.wixsite.com/nanhaipoetrypainting*, where you will find the poems and paintings accompanied with musical selections for a very unique experience.

简介

在卢沟桥事变爆发的那一年,作者出生于中国广东省南海县。在长达十四年的抗日侵略战争结束前,作者在中国四川省成都市郊区度过了他的童年。1945年抗日战争结束后,作者随家人移居台湾,并分别于1960年和1963年获得台湾大学哲学学士学位和哲学硕士学位。

1966年,作者前往美国在田纳西州立理工大学学习,并获得工程力学硕士学位。1970年毕业后,作者起初在肯塔基州任桥梁设计工程师,之后在不同州和不同城市的多家公司工作过,主要从事计算机编程和分析工作。

早在1969年,作者和王川培小姐结婚,随着岁月的流逝,四个孩子先后出生: 美生、力生、宜生和华生。作者目前居住在加利福尼亚州雷东朵海滩市,他写诗、作画(使用微软画笔创作)并欣赏古典音乐,还热衷于研究天文学以及错综复杂的全球关系。

Brief Biography

The author was born in Nanhai County, Guangdong Province, China, in the year of the Marco Polo Bridge Incident. Before the end of the 14-year War of Resistance against Japanese Aggression, he also spent his childhood in the outskirts of Chengdu, in the Sichuan province of China. After the war, his family relocated to Taiwan in 1945, where he remained until he graduated from Taiwan University with a B.A. and M.A. in Philosophy, in 1960 and 1963 respectively.

In 1966, the author traveled to the United States to continue his studies at Tennessee Technological University, where he obtained an M.S. in Engineering Mechanics. After graduating in 1970, he began working as a bridge design engineer in the State of Kentucky. For years to come the author worked for various companies in different cities and states, mainly employed in the field of computer programming and analysis.

In 1969 the author married Miss Wang Chuanpei, and together they had four children—Frank, Sebastian, Andy and Michael. The author currently resides in Redondo Beach, California, where he spends his time writing poems, creating digital illustrations (Microsoft Paint), and listening to classical music. He also has a passion for astronomy as well as the intricacies of global relations.

致谢

　　在此, 我衷心感谢我的妹妹陈湘云、我的家人以及我的好朋友在我创作的过程中给予的支持和指导。

　　感谢陈华生、Satya Senesac和Sarah Simmonds把中文诗准确恰当地翻译成英文诗, 感谢他们的辛勤努力与付出。

　　最後感谢陈力生为本书提供创作封面设计, 书名, 和简述。

Acknowledgements

I would like to express my sincere gratitude to my younger sister Chen Xiangyun, my family, and my close friends for offering their support and guidance throughout my creative process.

I would also like to extend my gratitude to Michael Chen, Satya Senesac, and Sarah Simmonds for their dedication to properly translating the Chinese poems into English.

Finally I would like to thank Sebastian Chen for his masterful work in designing the cover, composing the title, and writing the blurb for the book.

诗篇

Poems

一只小鸟

2008年10月09日

A Little Bird

October 09, 2008

爱出自真情
哪能轻易地挂在口边?

深深地隐藏在心中
说出去像小鸟飞失在雾中

小鸟在笼窗后仰望
向往白云碧天

无边的草原
翠绿的森林
开阔宏伟的湖山

有那么一天
心中窗口会开放
尽情地翱翔在蓝天

Love comes from one's true feelings
How could it then be expressed so casually?

It is hidden deeply in the heart
Love spoken out loud is like a bird lost in the fog

The little bird looking out from within its cage
Aspires to the white clouds and blue skies

The boundless prairies
The lush green forests
The magnificent hills and lakes

One day
The window of the heart will open
And the bird will eagerly soar into the sky

秋叶

2010年11月02日

Autumn Leaves

November 02, 2010

阳光明媚的春天里
绿青的树叶守护着枝梢上含苞待放的花朵

一天清早
迎着春风
花儿在薄雾笼罩的晨曦向曙光炫耀绽放

而今
那些苍白的花瓣儿
一片片在微风里悠荡飘零
随山涧溪流漂逝

秋风里那片落寞的叶儿
也终于从树梢轻轻地飘落山谷树旁的小溪
宁静却聚神地仰望着树梢搜寻着记忆

暴风急雨的深秋
严冬的寒冻冰封之后
一个早春

满树的花蕾
花儿竞艳

During the sunny, enchanting season of spring
A tree's green leaves guard budding flowers on the tips of its branches

One early morning
Greeting the spring breeze
The flowers in the misty morning light show off to the dawn

Now
Those pale petals
Sway and fall in the breeze
Drifting away down the mountain stream

A lonely leaf in the autumn wind
Finally falls gently from the tree into a creek in the valley
Quietly he looks up and focuses on the treetop searching his memory

After a stormy late autumn
And a freezing cold winter
Early spring arrives

Flower buds bloom all over the tree
Competing with one another's beauty

一片枯缩的秋叶
在清澈的溪底
情深地仰慕搜寻着百花丛中
那朵曾经最亮丽的花朵

A shriveled leaf
In the bed of the clear creek
Looks up admiringly searching deep within his heart
For the most beautiful flower among them all

木棉花开的季节

2011年06月02日

Kapok Season

June 02, 2011

夜空众星闪烁
草丛中是闪烁舞动的流萤飞虫
那一团团绿色的光芒
带领着我乘着风之羽
梦回幼儿时光

木棉花开的季节
遍布丘陵中满地橙红的花
一朵朵一簇簇似一团团燃烧的烈火

初夏傍晚的后院和哥哥妹妹
仰望夜空
数着点点繁星
含着棒棒糖
扇着小扇儿
听妈妈绘声绘色地讲述着安徒生童话故事

今宵
夜凉如水
那依旧闪亮的星星是母亲的眼睛依然带着牵挂

Stars twinkle in the evening sky
Fireflies flicker and dance in the grass
Their radiant green glow
Leads me to ride the feathers of the wind
And dream back to my childhood

It is kapok season
The hills are filled with orange-red blossoms
One by one they form a cluster of flowers resembling flames

An early summer evening in the backyard with my sister and brother
Looking up at the night sky
Counting the stars
Lollipops in our mouths
Waving hand fans
Listening to Mother vividly tell a Hans Christian Andersen fairy tale

Tonight
The evening is cool
The stars still sparkle like Mother's caring eyes

四月天

2008年03月31日

April Day

March 31, 2008

闪电撕裂夜空
雷雨轰破宁静
谁,摧毁了虚弱又残破的爱?
粉碎的心灵
伴随着极端的愤怒与绝望
余留下无尽的哀伤…

当狂风鞭打着巨浪
豪雨洗刷着壮丽山河后

微风会安抚着宁静的湖水
阳光会亲吻着绿荫大地
鸟儿会歌唱着春天的欢呼

当春风吹起千草
千草浮起百花

万紫千红的四月天会远吗?

Lightning rips apart the night sky
Thunderstorms blast through the tranquility
Who destroyed this feeble and dilapidated love?
A shattered soul
Filled with rage and despair
All that remains is endless grief...

After mighty winds whip up giant waves
After heavy rains wash off the mountains and rivers

The breeze will calm the quiet lake
The sun will kiss the green earth
The birds will sing the cheers of spring

When the spring breeze blows across a thousand blades of grass
And the grass holds up hundreds of flowers

Could a sunny April day be far away?

思念

2010年06月11日

Longing

June 11, 2010

傍晚彩云里的夕阳
在墙上徐徐地往上延伸
终于静静地吻着妳的笑容

孤寂的室内
那悠扬的音符伴随着
妳我又再飞越时空的彩虹
　到最初相识的日子

是春夏的艳阳
　凤凰花下
　听风声虫鸣

是微风拂面的秋日
　蜿蜒起跌的山丘小径上
　满山的枫叶红似火

是初冬寒夜
　校舍窗外雪花飘零
　路灯下似蝴蝶婆娑起舞

回忆妳甜蜜的笑容
优美的歌声

The sun set amidst colorful clouds
Its light slowly climbed up the wall
Until it quietly kissed your smile

In the lonely room
With a melody to accompany us
You and I flew over the rainbow of time and space
    to the first time we met

It is early summer and the sun is shining beautifully
    We are listening to the songs of the wind and the insects
    underneath a phoenix flower tree

It is a breezy autumn day
    We are on a little winding road rising up and down the hills
    surrounded by fiery red maple leaves

It is a cold winter night
    We are watching snowflakes flutter like dancing butterflies
    beneath a street lamp outside your dorm window

I can see your sweet smile
I can hear your beautiful singing

弹奏钢琴奏鸣曲
那扣人心弦的情景

那么朦胧
又多么遥远了
那些远去的岁月啊
如梦似幻

How you played that piano sonata
The memory tugs at my heartstrings

Now everything is hazy
So very distant
Those years of youth have long since passed
Like a dream or fantasy

足 迹

2007年12月03日

Footprints

December 03, 2007

沐浴在闪光片片的浅海
珊瑚群多姿多彩的身段在流光中灿烂
灿烂是春风带动万紫千红百花缤纷

鱼儿成群结队在蔚蓝色流光中来去匆匆赴宴
赴宴是灯红酒绿嘈杂夜市的闲人

而,千万年后
满天焚火
青山烧尽
河湖干涸
留下是城镇浩劫后的破墙废墟

是时光,是生物的时钟,追逐最后的永恒
永恒刻藏在高山岩层化石中

而,阳光会再孕育幸存余生的珊瑚
如大地万劫新生的幼芽迎接甘露

人类的足迹会再重现
如很久很久以前吗?

Bathed in the shining shallows near the shore
The colorful coral that shimmers in the undercurrent is brilliant
Brilliant are the flowers aroused by the spring wind

Schools of fish scurry beneath the glowing azure light to a lavish feast
Feasting crowds gather at a boisterous night market

After a few hundred thousand years
The sky will be aglow from sweeping fires
Forested mountains will burn down
Rivers and lakes will dry up
City walls will be reduced to rubble in the Great Disaster

Time—the biological clock—chases eternity
Eternity engraved within layers of fossils beneath the mountains

Eventually sunlight will breathe new life into the surviving coral
And new sprouts will greet the sweet morning dew

Will mankind's footprints appear once again
As they did long ago?

夕阳红

2007年11月12日

Red Sunset

November 12, 2007

为什么时光不能回流
流回到青春的年代
为什么要去爱
爱在夕阳红的傍晚

梦回曾经属于自己的天地
那个时代多么古老遥远啊

年轻得像草原上的俊马
美丽得像含滴早春的玫瑰
纯真得像婴儿天真的笑颜

眼前
只见落日晚霞红遍天
天边星星泪光闪闪

渐渐地
默默地
退了光彩

终于
漆黑笼罩了一切…

Why can't time flow backward
Flow backward to the age of youth
Why are we compelled to love
Love during our red sunset

Dreaming of a time the world once belonged to me
A time so long ago and far away

Spry like a young horse in the prairie
Beautiful like a dew-covered rose in early spring
Pure like the innocence in a baby's smile

Now
Sunset's glow spreads across the sky
And stars twinkle like tears on the horizon

Gradually
Silently
The colors of the sunset fade

Finally
The pitch-black sky consumes everything…

大地震

<献给四川震灾中英勇的人们>

2008年05月29日

Catastrophic Earthquake

Dedicated to the Heroes of the Great Sichuan Earthquake

May 29, 2008

刹那间
天摇地动
嘶声喊叫中
跌落深处

破墙断梁紧压着身子
如千刀切割
尘土扑面欲喘不能
声嘶力竭后
微弱的呻吟
然后是死寂的平静

醒来是冰冷无边的黑暗
饥饿、疼痛、惊吓、
绝望了…

半昏迷中似乎见到
近处的小溪流水
远方的绿林山丘
在蓝天白云阳光下
春风吹皱着千草野花

是狂风暴雨的盛夏
是秋色中起舞的枫叶

Suddenly
The sky rocks and the earth convulses
Amidst the screaming and shouting
I fall into the depths

Broken beams and walls press against my body
Like a thousand knives slicing into me
Dust covers my face and I struggle to breathe
Exhausted from crying out
I faintly moan
And then yield to dead silence

After waking to endless cold darkness
I am overcome by hunger, pain, and fear
I despair...

Delirious, I seem to glimpse
A flowing brook nearby
Green wooded hills far away
White clouds and sunshine beneath blue skies
A spring breeze forming waves across the grasses and wildflowers

A stormy hot summer
Maple leaves dancing in autumn

是初冬雪飘宁静的夜晚
　和父母天伦欢乐的日子

不知醒睡了
　多少个余震的日夜
时间似乎停止在永恒的黑夜中

耳边听到呼叫声
断墙破了
强烈的光线射入
带着人们的欢呼声

在瓦砾废墟
闪烁的星夜下
正向着生命奔驰

Snowflakes floating on a quiet winter night
    happy to be among family

I pass between wakefulness and sleep
    through countless days and nights of aftershocks
Time seems to stop in the eternal darkness

Suddenly, I hear yelling all around me
A crack appears in the wall
And a strong beam of light shoots in
Bringing in the cheers of people

My weak body is placed on a stretcher
In the shimmering rubble and ruin beneath the starry night sky
I am rushed toward life

无奈

2009年08月18日

Apathy

August 18, 2009

在忙碌厌烦的日子
且让无奈失神的眼
给窗外北风
涂抹彩墨

涂大海深蓝
抹上淡淡蓝天浮云
海鸥飞翔

添上初冬雪花飘飞
雪花轻点斜坡
枫林红似火

请让海鸥衔走
把一片片的无奈
散落浪花中

After a busy day of boredom
Divert your apathetic and inattentive eyes
To paint the north wind outside the window
With something colorful

Paint a deep blue sea
A pale blue sky with floating clouds
And a soaring seagull

Paint drifting snow in the winter
Snowflakes gently touching sloping hillsides
Filled with maple trees as red as fire

Please have the seagull pick up all the apathy
Piece by piece
And scatter it among the waves

梦幻

2014年10月09日

Fantastical Dream

October 09, 2014

月色灿烂的星光下
忆起了一箩筐滴漏的记忆

恒古闪烁的银河岸边
去寻找流浪迷失的星星

烧尽的青春似余烬轻轻飘逝
拭去一层层淡薄的灰
有泪的留痕

那丢失已久的怀念
像残留的花瓣风雨中
散落在梦里的思愁

而黄昏夕阳中
悄悄溜走的身影
已被无声的海风吹散

The moonlight shines magnificently beneath resplendent stars
As I recollect a basket of leaking memories

At the edge of the everlasting, twinkling Milky Way
I search for wandering lost stars

Burnt-out youth gently drifts away like embers
I wipe off a thin layer of gray ash
Revealing traces of tears

Long-lost memories
Like fallen petals in a storm
Scatter into the anguish of my dream

As sunset fades into dusk
My shadow quietly escapes
Blown away by a soundless sea breeze

妳为什么走了

2008年12月24日

Why Did You Leave Us

December 24, 2008

妳为什么仓促地走了?
明知是一条不归之路啊!
而今绿草浓荫环抱着妳
玫瑰也在晨雾冷风中悲泣

妳为什么静静地走了?
明知永别孩儿和我啊!
今早细雨朦胧沐浴着妳
鸟儿也在寒冻中颤抖

妳非要走吗?
在无星的夜里
明知气息会止,血液会凝啊!
今晚夜色深沉
只有风雨依伴抚爱着妳

妳可听到我内心悲痛地千呼万唤?
妳可听到我心灵深处痛苦地哀求?

我俩情深似海
合力养育孩儿成人
同心一致　搏斗坎坷命运
期待有朝一日驱除病魔

Why did you leave us so suddenly?
You knew it was a road from which you could never return
Now the woods and green grass surround you
Even the roses shed tears in the bitter cold wind

Why did you leave us so quietly?
You knew you would never see us again
Now hazy drizzle bathes you in the morning
Even the little birds tremble upon the treetops

Did you really have to go?
In the starless night
You knew your breath would cease and your blood would congeal
Tonight the darkness is so heavy
Now only the wind and rain accompany and care for you

Do you hear the agonizing cries deep within my heart?
Do you hear the bitter pleas deep within my soul?

We were so much in love
We raised our children together
We struggled on a difficult journey towards our fate
Expecting to conquer the illness someday

不是妳的错
不幸的是妳的血统选择了妳
妳只能默默忍受
而今虽躺下
但妳从未被击倒过

如今妳已先走了
请等着啊!
生命原是短暂

那一天终将来到
那一天啊!
我俩再重逢直到永远永远…

It was not your fault
Your lineage unfortunately chose you
You could only suffer in silence
Now you lie down
But you were never defeated

You took your leave first
Please wait for me!
Life is so very short

The day will finally come
Someday
We will meet again and be together forever...

团圆

2009年02月04日

Reunion

February 04, 2009

海风携带着白云
金色朝阳在蓝天蔓延

带着忧伤,他又来了
亲了我的脸轻声叹息
泪珠从花瓣上滑落

花开,花谢…
很久没见他来

啊!看呀!
脚边墓旁
新雕的名字在闪耀微笑
焕发出永恒的光彩

The sea breeze carries white clouds
As the golden morning sun spreads across the blue sky

With sadness he visits again
He kisses my face and softly sighs
Teardrops slip down my petals

Flowers bloom, flowers wither...
I haven't seen him for quite some time

Hey, look!
On the tomb next to my feet
A newly engraved name shines and smiles
Radiating brilliance for all eternity

失去的青春

2009年06月29日

Lost Youth

June 29, 2009

妳轻轻地走来
走出我的梦
梦中的迷茫思念

妳带来似曾相识的少女
青春隐藏在妳依然苗条的身影

那失落的情意
　　是夜雨院校
　　遮掩伞下私语

昔往的真纯
　　是夜雾昏暗路灯
　　树影中的搂抱

今朝
依然是沙滩上海水的清凉
和那追逐着游船海鸥的豪情

我俩靠肩滩上
遥望搜寻海天之外
那永不回来的青春

Gently you walk towards me
Emerging from my dream
A dream filled with confusion and longing

You bring with you the young lady I once knew
Traces of youth emanate from your slim figure

Our lost affection
    remains in the whispers of that rainy night
    underneath the umbrella at our college campus

Our past innocence
    remains in the embrace of that foggy night
    beneath the dimly lit shadows

Today
The water along the sandy beach is still cool
A passionate seagull chases a small boat

We sit shoulder-to-shoulder on the beach
Searching beyond the sea and sky
For youth that will never return

泡沫

2010年01月22日

Foam

January 22, 2010

气泡在空中漂浮

五颜六色泛流融汇出
　　高楼大厦林立
　　如参天红木森林
　　地面行人车辆
　　如过江之鲫

而灰色暗淡淤泥混流显示着
　　烟火满城
　　破墙碎壁
　　战争残酷
　　家破人亡

太平盛世
烽火连城
都会像气泡霎眼破灭消失

地球之于无穷无限
一直加速膨胀
数十亿年的宇宙

如肥皂泡
只片刻显现

Bubbles floating in the air

Shiny colors run together to form
    High-rise buildings far and wide
    Climbing the sky like redwood forests
    Pedestrians and vehicles swarming the ground
    Like carp thronging across a river

A dull gray muddy mixture reveals
    Cities ablaze
    Broken walls
    The brutality of war
    Destroyed homes and families

Peace and prosperity
War and calamity
Like a bursting bubble, they will suddenly disappear

The Earth lives in an infinite universe
That has been accelerating in its expansion
For billions of years

Like a bubble of soap
It exists for only a moment

暮岁

2012年06月01日

Twilight Years

June 01, 2012

又一次梦回童年
满天闪烁的星星
不知什么引来凄然惨淡愁月色

一群萤火虫
　携带着小灯笼缭绕儿时梦
深夜带引我寻找家乡的归路

一路走过来
在喧闹繁忙的城镇
像游牧族群逐水草迁离
只为寻找一线生存的间隙

伤怀记忆的痕迹
沧桑寂寥哀愁的岁月
也逐渐褪了色彩

不经意地
已从青春走进了
落寞伤感孤寂的暮岁

Once again I dreamed of childhood
A sky full of twinkling stars
I don't know what led the moonlight to appear so sad and gloomy

In my childhood dream
A group of fireflies carrying small lanterns surround me
Deep in the night they guide me in search of the road home

I traveled a long way
Enduring the hustle and bustle of small towns and big cities
Like a nomad chasing grass and water
Searching for the edge of survival

The traces of wounding memories
And vicissitudes from my lonesome sorrowful years
Have gradually lost their color

Inadvertently
I stepped out of my youth and into
My sad and lonely twilight years

燕子,飞走吧!

2010年10月22日

Swallow, Fly Away!

October 22, 2010

请飞走吧!
我也终于要离开的
寒舍滴漏
大风里摇摆抖动
不值得留守了

冷风秋雨阵阵袭来
吹散了旧情片片飞扬
像秋天的落叶随风漂泊在溪水上
让往事回忆随流水消逝

夏末的花儿也已凋零
光秃枝桠突显秋色萧瑟
严寒随雪花即将来临

啊!燕子
别带着内疚与歉意
飞往远方的春天
寻觅风和日丽、鸟语花香

Please fly away!
At long last, I too want to leave
This humble, run-down shack
It leaks and wobbles in the wind
It is not worth it to remain

Relentless cold wind and autumn rain whip down
Blowing away old affections
Like falling leaves in the wind that stray into the creek
Let memories of the past float away and perish

Late summer's flowers have withered
Bare branches depict the bleakness of autumn
A severe winter will soon bring a snowstorm

O swallow
Do not feel guilty or be sorry
Fly to the distant spring
Seek a sunny day where the birds sing and the flowers are fragrant

青藏高原

2011年08月04日

The Qinghai-Tibet Plateau

August 04, 2011

我看见
　　高铁列车的窗外
　　藏羚羊群奔跑在起伏的草原上

我闻到
　　原野气息
　　油菜花的飘香扑面而来

我聆听
　　强风暴雨敲打撞击车窗
　　高架铁桥下的急流

我感受
　　来自湖上彩云的寒冷薄雾
　　秋末初冬日落湖中彩霞的晖映

云雾缭绕高山雪峰
峡谷冻土冰川
风雪交加寒气袭人
我的心　飞啊！
翱翔在青藏高原上

I see
>   Through the window of a high-speed train
>   A herd of antelope dashing across a vast prairie

I smell
>   The breath of the wilderness
>   The fragrance of canola flowers wafting into my face

I hear
>   A powerful rainstorm striking the windows
>   Rapids gushing underneath the high bridge

I feel
>   The cool mist of the colorful clouds above the lake
>   Reflecting the late autumn, early winter sunset

Clouds and fog surround snow-covered alpine peaks
Canyons, permafrost, and glaciers
Wind and snow form a bone-chilling assault
My heart soars!
Hovering above the Qinghai-Tibet Plateau

涟漪波纹

2011年08月09日

Ripples and Waves

August 09, 2011

那个年代
妳我有不可抗衡的灾难与不幸

风雨中
娇艳的花自花丛中坠下
翠色欲滴的叶儿也从枝头脱落

多少个寒冬已随雪花飘逝?

如今
心底被吹皱
一池春水
唤醒千条涟漪波纹

咱们
是否会像萤火虫
闪烁夜空?

又是否
最终
瞬间
消失踪影?

That year
You and I faced unavoidable disaster and misfortune

In the wind and rain
Elegant flowers fell from their bushes
Brilliant emerald leaves separated from their branches

How many winters have followed the path of snowflakes and drifted away?

Now
My heart is like a pond
Touched by the spring breeze
Awakening a thousand ripples and waves

Will we be like fireflies
Illuminating the night sky
With a sparkling glow?

Will we
Finally
In an instant
Disappear without a trace?

初雪

2010年12月22日

Early Snow

December 22, 2010

初冬
雪花飘飞覆盖着山丘小坡
涂绘出一片白茫茫
白雪蔽匿不住枝梢梅花点点红
唤起我的回忆
往昔雪白稚气的童年

折一枝梅花
沿着雪片飘扬林园的小径
追逐着寒风里纷纷飘落的雪片
栖息在池塘荷叶残枝上的蜻蜓

爬上树枝捉颤抖的小雀
和雪堆残叶里的小虫
冻红了脸颊双手

啊！梦憧的童年
未了的儿时梦

Early winter
Snowflakes cover the small slopes of the hillsides
Painting a vast white expanse
The snow fails to conceal pockets of little red plum blossoms
The scene stirs my memories
To recall the snow white innocence of my childhood

I break off a branch of plum flowers
Following a snow-flurried trail through the woodland park
I chase snowflakes that drift down one after another in the cold wind
Dragonflies perch on broken lotus branches in the pond

I climb a tree and catch a tiny, trembling bird
Insects lie covered under decayed leaves in piles of snow
My flushed face and small hands remain frozen

Alas! My unfinished childhood dreams
Unfulfilled are the dreams of childhood

山火

2007年12月18日

Mountain Fire

December 18, 2007

在起伏山坡的丛林里
一栋栋的房屋
映辉了夕阳秋色姹紫嫣红

而急噪的风
如千军万马
奔腾追逐着逃窜林中的火点

烈火烧毁了
　家宅园林
　　和每一个梦

家园在激热的情
火红的爱中
声斯嚎叫

最终化为白烟灰烬…

In the jungle of rolling hills and trees
A line of houses stood side by side
The sunset reflected spectacular autumn hues

Then, an impatient wind
Like an army of soldiers and horses
Swiftly chased a fleeing fire into the hills

The fire burned down
    all the homes and gardens
    along with every dream

Houses burned in ecstasy
With a fiery passion
They screamed and howled

Finally everything turned to white smoke and gray ash…

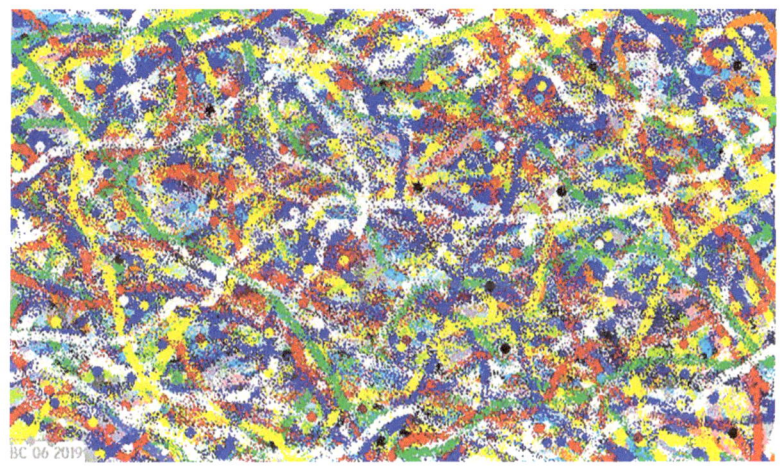

交会

2009年11月04日

Rendezvous

November 04, 2009

妳我相识在网络
交会在无影虚幻光纤中
心绪也曾经
　　如花灿烂
　　如海澎湃

而今
在这雪飘寒冷孤独的黑夜里
送上一盏微笑关怀
啜饮一点温暖
但温情会循随
　　时光的暗流撕灭

那彩画上迷茫暧昧的情意
最终也会像昙花
瞬间凋萎

You and I met on the internet
We rendezvoused in shadowless virtual fiber
Our affection was
    like a blooming flower
    like a surging ocean wave

Now
On this snowy, frigid, and lonely night
I send you a small cup of smile and concern
So you can sip a little bit of warmth
However, the warm feeling will follow
    the undercurrent of time and vanish

Your colorful paintings are filled with confused and ambiguous feelings
At last those feelings will be like the epiphyllum oxypetalum
And instantly wither

洛矶山群

2007年07月29日

The Rocky Mountains

July 29, 2007

迎面是一座座断崖与延绵不绝的青翠杉
清澈弯曲的溪流潺潺滑过
片片白云
　　悬挂在如洗万里的晴空
细瀑如千条丝在斜壁上映照着银光
沙质岩被融雪
　　冲洗成一排排的兵马俑
远见山羊在斜岩秃壁俯瞰
　　近处白尾鹿奔驰在丛林中
垂直陡峭的岩壁挺撑了千万年

永恒的是尖峭耸峙银白的山峰
　　是崇山峻岭雪盖的悬崖
　　是流不尽的溪谷瀑布
　　是化不尽的亿万年冰河

澄静透澈碧绿的湖面似镜
　　倒映着冰雪覆盖的雪峰
水晶般剔透的蓝色湖泊
　　相互辉映着白雪皑皑的悬崖峭壁
樱粟花在微风
　　和蜂鸟穿梭中招展着衣裙
点动了山光水色
　　和湖边的青草百花

On the face of a cliff, a chain of green cedar stretches out
Clear water in winding streams gurgle and rush by
Patches of white clouds
    hang in otherwise clear skies for thousands of miles
Thin silver waterfalls shine like fine silk along inclined rocky walls
Sandy rocks washed off by melted snow
    turn into rows of Terracotta warriors
On sloping bald rock walls mountain goats overlook
    white-tailed deer galloping in the nearby jungle
These vertical sheets of rock have endured for millions of years

Eternal are the sharp silver and white peaks
    the mountain cliffs covered in snow
    the endless streams from the valley waterfalls
    the glaciers that millions of years could not melt

Mirror-like turquoise lakes
    reflect snow-covered peaks
Crystal blue lakes
    illuminate white snow-capped cliffs
Poppies show off their dresses
    while the breeze and hummingbirds shuttle back and forth
Revitalizing the mountainous landscape
    and its lakeside grasses and flowers

与游人漫步湖畔的小径衬托出一幅人间仙景
水气似雾又似云迷漫浮游在群山峡谷中
像少女的白纱裙在翡翠湖面上轻飘而过
傍晚的夕阳喷射出金光万丈
照映着远处的金壁群峰

别了啊　雄伟壮丽的洛矶山群！
愿你永永远远长驻千古万年

Visitors walk through the lakeside trails to experience a fairyland
Mist, like a fog or cloud, floats through the mountains and canyons
It buoyantly glides across the emerald lake like a flowing white skirt
The evening sunset emanates a lofty golden light
Highlighting the distant peaks and mountain walls

Farewell, majestic Rocky Mountains
May you reside for all eternity

永恒的真理

2016年04月23日

Eternal Truth

April 23, 2016

晚秋枝头上的残瓣
于风中抹着一层初霜
颤抖哆嗦摆晃欲堕
等候生命的终结
瞬间的引力下
下坠是生命的宿命

凡人的辩论不足论判
哲学语义仅不过是一厢情愿
只有验证能够诠释真实性
而科学在不停地自我更新
世上哪有永恒的真理?

In late autumn, flower petals wither on their branches
The wind paints on the first layer of frost
Shivering, trembling, and swaying
The leaves await the end of life
In an instant they succumb to gravity
Falling is the fate of life

Debates of men cannot determine truth
Philosophical arguments are just wishful thinking
Truth is verified by evidence
Yet science continues to evolve
So how can eternal truth exist in this world?

天山雪莲

2012年01月17日

The Tianshan Snow Lotus

January 17, 2012

神话中仙女撒落的奇异花
叶片花瓣宛若绵球
犹如穿上黄白绒衣

千百年来各族牧民
视雪莲花为爱的象征圣洁的化身

殊不知为何
雪莲花生长在
山峰严酷风雪交加
石壁冰渍岩缝碎石之中

朝霞落日染透燃烧天边
搏霜斗雪顽强地生存

宁愿孤芳自赏
傲视天下万草千花
挺立于天山雪峰之上

啊！
仅为在虎踞龙盘的高山
终年冰冻的悬崖陡壁上
镶嵌铺陈一片傲气和春色？

Mythological fairies sprinkled down these exotic flowers
The leaves and petals resemble a cotton ball
Wearing a yellow and white furry coat

For thousands of years herdsmen of all ethnic groups
Treated the snow lotus as a symbol of love and holy incarnation

Little did they know
The snow lotus grows
Through harsh blizzards and storms on snow-capped peaks
In the moraine and gravel crevices of rocky cliffs

As dusk and dawn dye the horizon with burning colors
The lotuses endure tenaciously, fighting frost and snow

Preferring to be alone and enjoy their own excellence
Looking down with disdain at all the other flowers
They stand tall on the snowy peaks

Wow!
Is it out of pride that you display your beauty
Only in high mountain tiger lairs and dragon caves
On frozen cliffs and icy slopes?

树苗棚

2011年01月03日

Greenhouse

January 03, 2011

坚挺的木架树苗棚饱受
　　白炽烈日烫热的灼晒
　　倾盆暴雨
　　狂风的鞭打
只为萌生的幼芽得以安然生长

春去
夏至
秋离
冬临

年复一年
树苗逐渐成长壮硕
枝桠展现葱郁的绿叶

终于是移植的时候
枯老朽木已身躬背驼
早已失去了昔日的执意、坚决与光泽

然而平静地
在带有寒意的秋风里
仰首微笑迎着灿烂的阳光
遥望着远处
红遍小山丘斜坡上的枫林

The strong wooden greenhouse endures
    blistering hot rays from the scorching sun
    torrential downpours
    furious whipping winds
Solely for the peaceful burgeoning of young saplings

Spring departs
Summer arrives
Autumn flees
Winter descends

Year after year
The saplings gradually grow stronger
Their branches begin to show lush green leaves

At last the time to transplant arrives
The old decaying wooden frame slumps in a hunchback
Its previous durability, shine, and determination long lost

And yet quietly
In the cold autumn wind
It lifts its head smiling to greet the bright sunshine
Gazing into the distance
At a red sea of maple trees on the slopes of a small hill

在风中一大片的枫叶
　　正朝着他摇旗呐喊欢呼

Fluttering in the wind, countless maple leaves
    wave their flags and cheer for the greenhouse

bc 05 2021

暴风雪

2011年11月21日

Snowstorm

November 21, 2011

冬天
风雪给大地绘画

树木丛林穿着白棉袄
草坪换了白地毯
河畔银树挂满亮耳环
在风雪中叮铃摇晃闪耀

冬天
我给风雪绘画

狂风大雪扫荡乡镇
白棉似的雪花满盖了屋顶街道
车辆滑边
机场瘫痪

肆虐的风雪啊!
亲人好友焦急忧心地等待一年一度的团圆相聚

During winter
Wind and snow paint the earth

Groves dressed in white padded winter coats
Lawns transformed into white carpet
Silver branches along the river dangling bright earrings
Clinking as they sway and sparkle in the wind and snow

During winter
I paint the snowstorm

Powerful gales and heavy snow sweeping the countryside
Cotton-like white snow blanketing the rooftops and streets
Vehicles skidding on the roadside
Paralyzed airports

What a raging blizzard!
Family and friends anxiously await their annual gathering

天塌了

2009年02月18日

The Sky Has Collapsed

February 18, 2009

没料到天塌了
别担心
我两脚立地
两手撑天

把重担放下吧
像蝴蝶翩翩起舞
在微风日晒的春天

近于完美无瑕的心灵
能承受那么多的不幸和苦难?
我真诚地祝福她有美满幸福的归宿

果有一天
她身心疲惫
别忘记
遥远的天边
有个地方
等待着妳归来

I didn't expect the sky to collapse
Don't worry
I will stand up on my feet
And hold the sky up with my hands

Let go of all your burdens
Like butterflies dancing gracefully
In the breeze and sunshine of spring

How can such a pure heart
Bear so much misfortune and suffering?
I sincerely hope that you find true happiness with someone

Perhaps one day
If you are physically and emotionally spent
Don't forget
In the distant edge of the sky
There is a place
Waiting for your return

亲情

2011年01月14日

Family Affection

January 14, 2011

多年远在异国他乡
为学业生涯
忽视了家人的鸿雁往来

翻阅父亲遗留的诗篇
始知望穿秋水念子情深
不禁黯然泪下

孩子们成长离家各奔西东
也为事业生活奋斗挣扎
难得归来探望言欢

一如昔往
清凉孤寂的室内
夕阳徐慢地
　仰望壁上父母的笑容
伴随着悠扬的小提琴奏鸣曲
悄然地渐入梦乡

I remained in a foreign country for years
All for the sake of my studies and my career
Ignoring letters from home

It wasn't until I read through the poems my father left behind
That I realized how deeply he missed his son
I couldn't help but shed tears

My children have grown and left home
They likewise struggle for their careers and lives
Rarely returning home to spend quality time together

As always
Inside this cold and lonely room
The evening sun slowly looks up
    to a photo of my smiling parents hanging on the wall
Accompanied by the sorrowful melody of a violin sonata
I quietly and gradually drift into dreamland

小烛光

2015年03月17日

Tiny Candles

March 17, 2015

闪烁的银河里
咱们航行在不同的水道

一次无意的碰撞
爆发了一闪的灿烂
燃烧一瞬的温暖

仅片刻
彗星炯炯的泪珠已千万里
消失于深空了无踪影

千万年后
泪水已酵化酿造醇酒小光点

彗星托着千万颗小烛光
闪耀地划过天际的夜空

In the sparkling Milky Way galaxy
We sailed in different waterways

An unintentional collision
Exploded into a flash of brilliance
The burning created a momentary warmth

In an instant
The glistening tears of the comet were thousands of miles away
Disappearing into outer space without a trace

After many eons
The tears have fermented into small specks of light

The comet carries thousands of tiny candles
Shining and soaring across the night sky

无声之歌

2019年5月4日

Silent Song

May 04, 2019

希望我的诗影响传承给下一代
像黄河源头之急流瀑布
豪迈而壮丽冲刺奔流入大海

但是
我是一条沙漠的河流
短小的川流
生在沙漠
消失于沙漠中

对于大漠的渴望
用奔腾热血献上一生

我只有一个梦想
在白杨树的绿叶中
成千上万的绿色脉茎里
流淌着我惊涛骇浪无声之歌

I want my poetry to pass down to future generations
Like the gushing waterfalls at the source of the Yellow River
Magnificent and heroic rushing toward the sea

However
I am just a desert river
With a short and narrow stream
I was born in the desert
I will die in the desert

To the great barren land
I offer all of my life without reserve

I have only one dream
To flow inside the green leaves of the poplar tree
Within its thousands of veins
Amidst the silent song of my stormy waves

www.ingramcontent.com/pod-product-compliance
Lightning Source LLC
Chambersburg PA
CBHW042235090526
44589CB00001B/3